ARE YOU OKAY?

May Mokdad

Published by Mindstir Media, LLC
45 Lafayette Rd | Suite 181| North Hampton, NH 03862 | USA
1.800.767.0531 | www.mindstirmedia.com

Printed in the United States of America
ISBN-13: 978-1-960142-60-3

MINDSTIR MEDIA

This book is dedicated to my beautiful sister Hala who always saw the good in everyone and left us way too soon.

We buried my mom today. It is the worst day of my life. I feel so sad, scared, and lonely. Everything is different now and all people wanted to do is ask me how I am. No one wanted to talk about my mom and why she was gone. Most people disappeared altogether.

Instead, they would say things to make themselves feel better, "You need time." "I'm sorry for your loss." "Find your strength." "I will give you space" or "I'm here to help." And "Are you okay?" Nothing seemed to help me feel better. I had an extreme emptiness in my heart, and of course I wasn't okay! I was more confused than ever. I wanted to know why she died, how could she leave me when I still needed her so much? What if I did something differently? I had so many questions, and no answers, just pain.

No one could bare to talk about death to a child. So they didn't. I never felt more alone, even with everyone around me. Time seemed to be moving slowly and all I wanted was for my mom to be alive again. For most people life went on as usual, but I felt so heavy, tired, and sad. Simple things became so hard to complete. I wasn't motivated to jump back into life. I needed time to learn how to live without my mom. All I could to do was sleep in my bed and not talk to anyone.

The pain kept growing until it was too large to bare! A loud voice filled with such sadness yelled out "I WANT MY MOM BACK!!" I cried for hours, too weak to do anything else.

Nothing seemed to help until one day I met a girl named Huhu at school, who also lost her mom a year ago. She was all too familiar with grief and learned a few things that helped her feel better along the way. We talked about our pain and cried together. The first thing she said to me was, "tell me all about your mom." Most people wanted me to forget about what happened and go on with things as normal, so she took me by surprise.

Suddenly something in me woke up and I began to talk. "She is smart and very funny." "She loved to dance and loved the color yellow." Find me an unhappy person who wears yellow, you can't it's too happy of a color! "She wrote poetry about her life." "She loved nature and being around family." " She loved to travel and was very spontaneous." Oh and how much she loved dragonflies! She told their story of strength when one flew by. I just couldn't stop talking and crying at the same time, because I missed her so much! And she listened and listened. While I talked and talked.

Huhu came up with an idea, "why don't we do something to remember your mom?" I was excited again. We framed a picture of my mom and put a candle by it to light in the morning and at night. During that time, I talked about my favorite memories of her. How we walked on the beach and watched the sunset. When we cooked together and laughed. How much I miss running into the house to talk to her after school.

I started to feel better, but my heart still hurt. Huhu said, "that is your heart aching." She said, "you will feel it every time you miss your mom." My eyes started to swell with tears again and I began to write in a journal all my dreams of her, and each morning and night I talked to her picture while I lit a candle. Soon that was my routine, and the pain wasn't so strong. I felt like she was still in my life somehow.

But how do I get through a whole day without crying? A song, a smile, a birthday, a memory would trigger my tears. My friend said, "each tear is a moment you had with your mom, and you will cry for a long time to come." That is how your release the pain. But you will also learn when you are ready to move forward. Until then, "let those tears out, and you will feel better." She was right, soon I cried less and smiled more, but I never forgot my mom.

Each day that passed I remembered her through old pictures, her bracelet, or an action. A visit to the cemetery to tell her all that has happened to me. For Mother's Day, I planted yellow flowers and put a dragonfly garden stick to remind me that she is always nearby. She lives in my memories and through me. Huhu helped me remember the good times and how to deal with so many new feelings. It's okay to cry and talk about her even though she is gone. I have some peace now and I can cry whenever I miss her. I talk to her picture each day and when I'm outside I see her in the yellow flowers and dragonflies. I read my journal daily and always add to it after each dream. She is alive in my head and in my heart always with memories that are now treasures to me.

Huhu helped me find the strength to go on when I felt like I couldn't. Now if someone asks me are you okay, I simply say today I am because I will always remember my mom!

For those who have experienced a loss, grief is different for everyone and there is no timeline to heal. It is an unspeakable pain that hurts daily. Just know you are not alone, and it helps to talk to someone until you feel whole again. Sometimes it's the little things that help you when you need them the most. A thought, a memory, a good cry, a picture, an object, family, or friends. You will get back to some kind of normal but understand for each person the timeline is different, until then hold on to the great memories, those will never die.

CPSIA information can be obtained
at www.ICGtesting.com
Printed in the USA
BVHW011652240323
661107BV00002B/18